Snakes

Fun Facts & Amazing Pictures - Learn About Snakes

Spencer Jones

Disclaimer

All rights reserved. No part of this e-book may be reproduced or transmitted in any form or by any means, electronic or mechanical, including photocopying, recording, or by any information storage and retrieval system, without the expressed written permission from the author and publishing company.

The First Thing You Need to Know About Snakes

Snakes are reptiles; their closest relatives are the crocodiles and turtles. They do not have legs but have elongated bodies that are flexible. The shape of their body depends on the environment (they call this their habitat) that they live in.

Reptiles are cold-blooded animals. This means that they cannot control their body temperature. If snakes want to increase their body temperature, snakes expose themselves to the sun - they go sun bathing. If they want to lower their body temperature, they lie under the shadows.

Snake Body Parts

Snakes have bones. Their vertebrae ca be as few as 200 and can be as many as 400, compare that to humans with only 33 vertebrae. A snake's jaw is made for swallowing which means that the jaw should be flexible. That's why the jaw is made of tendons and muscles and not just bones just like mammals.

The vital organs of a snake are protected by its muscles and ribs. Because a snake is elongated, its organs are also elongated. The stomach is also elongated but it easily adjusts its length based on the food that the snake has swallowed.

Snakes are also covered by scales that they use to move thorough surfaces and for climbing, Since they don't have eyelids, they have special scales that cover their eyes.

Snake Anatomy

Home Is Where the Snake Is

There around 2900 snake species around the world and they can be found in almost any environment except for places where the ground is permanently frozen like at the poles. Sea snakes are found in tropical waters and are known to have the most toxic venoms. Snakes can also be found in deserts, forests, streams, lakes and oceans.

Most snakes like to live in places that are dark and cool and where food is most abundant. In the backyard, you would find them hiding under the mulch or old lumber. Shrubs and unkempt lawns are also perfect hiding places for snakes.

Snake in Natural Habitat

Snake Ssssenssssessss

Snakes breathe through their nostrils but they don't smell through them. Snakes smell through the Jacobson's organ; by picking up air molecules using their tongue and depositing the particles into the organ found in the roof of the mouth. The Jacobson's organ uses the particles to gather information to be used by the snake.

Snakes hear through their jaw. Since snakes don't have ears in the outside, the jaws pick up sound vibration from the environment and then transmit it to the inner ears. They also have touch receptors all over their body which is often used when snakes communicate with other snakes.

Garter Snake

Snake Movement

Snakes move in four different ways. They are namely - serpentine movement, side winding movement, concertina movement and caterpillar movement. Snake movement is determined by the kind of environment they are in.

The serpentine movement is the normal way snakes move and is S-shaped. The

Side winding movement is a movement a snake uses when it is on slippery or loose surfaces such as sand in the dessert.

The concertina movement is used by snakes when they are climbing.

And finally the caterpillar movement which is a slow and straight movement normally used by snakes when they are on grassy surfaces.

Grass Snake

Shedding the Skin

When snakes grow larger, their scales become too tight. As a result, they shed their scales in a process called molting. When molting, snakes are temporarily blind because their eye is also covered with scales. Snakes use the hard surface of a rock to break the scales in the head and along the mouth and then slide the skin off.

Molting has several functions in snakes. First is the replacement of the old skin. Secondly, parasites such as ticks are also removed. Lastly, molting helps in the snake's growth especially in the early stages of its life.

The Mouth

A snake's mouth is built for swallowing. So, in order for the jaw to open wide enough, the jaw is connected at the back of the snake's skull and not on the sides. The two sides of the jaw are not connected by bone but by a ligament that can also stretch.

The type of teeth that can be found inside a snake's mouth depends on whether the snake is venomous or non-venomous. Non-venomous snakes often have similarly-shaped teeth that are pointing inwards so that the snake can gave a better grip at its food. Venomous snakes have a pair of enlarged fangs in the upper part of its mouth. The venomous fang is hollow just like the needle of a syringe; the venom passes through the hole and is injected into the prey.

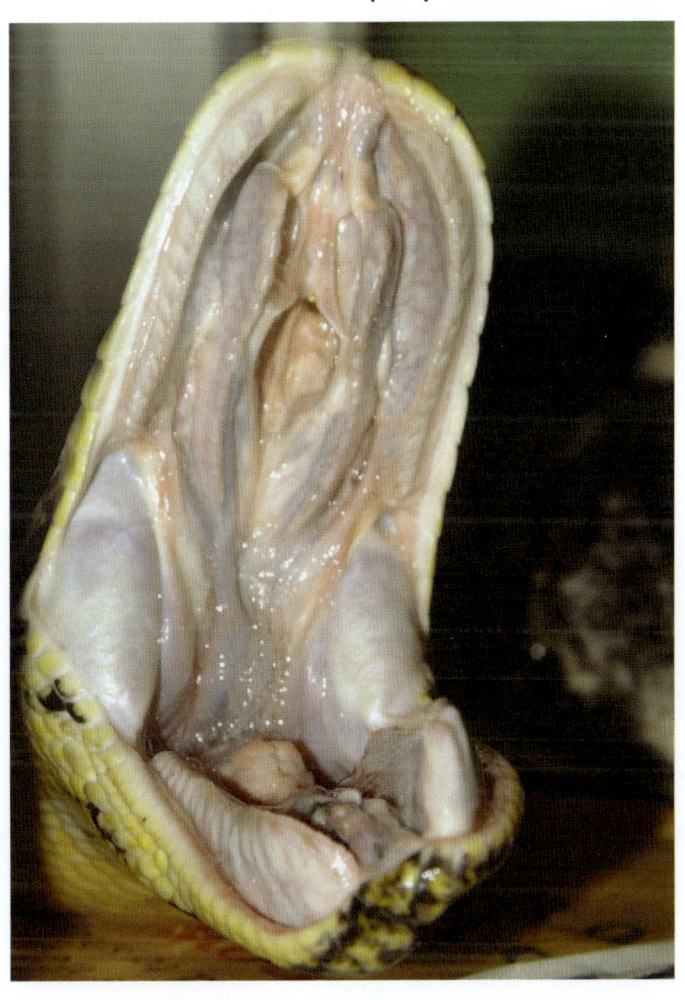

The Food We Eat

Snakes eat only meat (carnivores). Snakes can eat fish, snails, mammals such as rodents and deer, insects and even eggs. The size of the food depends on the size of the snake. A small anaconda for example will eat small insects and finish when it's small but will eventually eat large mammals like wild pigs and small crocodiles as an adult.

Snakes hunt for prey in a number of ways. The cantil snake has a yellow-tipped tail that looks like a worm. It uses its tail to attract birds. Some snakes in the dessert lie and wait under the sand to ambush small lizards.

The King cobra, on the other hand, only eats other snakes; while other snakes prefer to eat eggs. The food takes around 1 hour to move through the stomach and during this time, the snake lies still.

Snake Eating a Frog

Armed to the Teeth

Snakes have enemies too such as eagles, crocodiles, hawks, owls, coyotes and armadillos. Snakes also try to hide as much as possible to avoid detection. Some tropical snakes use their coloration to blend with their surroundings so their enemies will find it difficult to spot them. Others can burrow and hide themselves into the sand.

Rattlesnakes will rattle their tails violently to warn intruders. The cobra will raise its head and expand its hood to warn predators. Generally, most snakes will coil up when threatened

Rattle Snake in a Sticking Pose On a Warm Rock

Cuddling Without Arms – Snake Balls

Spring time is a busy period for some snakes such as the garter snake, the cottonmouth, and the anaconda. During this time, female snakes are ready for mating. However, female snakes only become ready for mating every 3 years and this results to a female snake being courted by a number of males.

This happens when females who are ready to mate leave scents on the ground as they crawl. This scent is picked up by male snakes which then follow the scent of the female snakes. More than a hundred male snakes will be able to pick up these scents called pheromones.

As a result, several male snakes swarm a single female snake resulting in snake balls. During this time, male snakes will not eat and will not even be aggressive. They will only be focused on mating and reproducing.

Royal Pyhton in His Egg

Rockabye Baby Snakes

The way baby snakes are brought into this world depends on the species of the snake. Some snakes are ovoviviparous which means that they keep their eggs inside their bodies and bring out baby snakes. Some snakes just lay eggs.

Snakes that lay eggs also vary in behavior. Some lay their eggs and just leave the eggs to hatch. Some like the King cobra will go as far as to make a nest for the eggs and even guard the eggs until they hatch. Pythons coil around their eggs to give them heat and help them incubate.

A Baby Green Tree Python

Anaconda

The Anaconda is largest and second longest snake in the world. They belong to the boa constrictor family and live in South America, particularly in the Amazon. Anacondas are great swimmers and like to stay near bodies of water to hunt for prey and to escape quickly.

When you talk about anacondas, you will most likely refer to the green anacondas of the Amazon. They can grow up to 29 feet and weigh more than 550 pounds. How did they become so big? They like to eat wild pigs, birds, turtles and jaguars.

Yellow Anaconda

Black Mamba

The Black Mamba is one of the most feared snakes in Sub-Saharan Africa. Experts consider it as the deadliest snake in the world and it is Africa's longest venomous snake with some reaching up to 14 feet in length. They are also among the fastest snakes in the world.

A Black Mamba will always try to avoid a confrontation but when cornered, it will raise its head and expand its hood much like a cobra. It will hiss loudly and will strike repeatedly at the intruder.

Black Mamba

Boa Constrictor

Boas are one of the largest snakes in the world and are non-venomous. Instead of injecting paralyzing venom, they constrict their prey until it can no longer breathe. Boa constrictors are often found in South America and are expert swimmers.

Depending on their environment, a Boa constrictor can be green, yellow, or red in color with different kinds of pattern in their back such as circles and diamonds. Boas like to dine on wild pigs, monkeys, birds, and almost anything they can catch. Boas can go up to 13 feet in length.

Boa Constrictor

Cobra

Cobras are among the most venomous snakes in the world. They are so called because of the hood that widens when they feel threatened. Cobras are found in Africa and in Asia.

The longest among the Cobras is the King Cobra. It can grow up to 18 feet in length and mostly eats other snakes. A single bite from a King Cobra contains enough venom to kill and elephant.

Cobra

Corn Snake

Corn snakes are most found in North America and are non-venomous. They mostly feed on rats that infest farms and are beneficial for humans. Corn snakes prefer overgrown fields, crowded forest floors, and abandoned buildings.

Corn snakes are among the most popular species of snake to take in as a pet. They can grow up to 4 to 6 feet in length and come in a variety of colors. Their reluctance to bite and calm attitude make them perfect pets.

Corn Snake

Garter Snake

Garter snakes are slightly venomous snakes and are found mostly in an area from North America all the way to Central America. They are also the only snake species found in Alaska. Garter snakes are carnivorous and would eat anything such as slugs, lizards and earthworms.

Garter snakes mate during spring and can form snake balls during the act. Female garter snakes give birth to live young. Upon birth, Garter snakes are ready to eat.

Garter Snake

Inland Taipan

The inland Taipan is one of the most venomous snakes in the world and is found in Australia. Depending on the season, they can be dark tan to dark green in color. They can grow to an average length of 1.8 meters or roughly 6 feet.

Inland Taipans like to eat small mammals such as rodents and birds. Like most snakes, the inland taipan prefers to escape the threat rather confront it. Inland Taipans can lay up to two dozen eggs and would usually lay them in abandoned burrows.

Inland Taipan

Python

Pythons are non-venomous and are the longest snakes in the world. They are mostly found in Africa and Asia. Pythons are very calm which makes them one of the most ideal and largest pet snakes to keep.

Burmese pythons have beautifully patterned skin. They are mostly found in the marshes of Southeast Asia and can grow up to 23 feet in length. Sadly, pythons are endangered because of the destruction of their habitat.

Royal Python Snake Rested on a wooden branch

Rattlesnake

Rattlers, as they are commonly called, are found mostly in the Americas. Rattlers are so-called because of the rattle that they make to warn predators. They can grow to between 3 to 4 feet in length.

Rattlers are venomous and will most often prey on rats and small birds. Rattlesnakes lie and ambush their prey or would sometimes go to their burrows and attack them. Although venomous, Rattlers will always stay away from humans.

Western Rattlesnake Strike Ready

Sea Snake

Sea snakes have flat tails just like a paddle to enable them to swim better. Their bodies are also flat to enable them to glide better in the water. They are also one of the most poisonous snakes in the world and are relatives of the Cobra.

Sea snakes are found in Africa, Asia and down to Australia. They prefer tropical waters where their bright color will blend with the rich corals of the tropics. They usually eat fish and eels.

Large Banded Sea Snake

Fun Facts

1. Just like fish, snakes don't have eyelids.

2. There are 2700 species of snakes, 375 of them are venomous.

3. Snake charming used to be a religious practice, now it's done for entertainment.

4. The Komodo Island in Indonesia has the most number of poisonous snakes per square meter than anywhere else on Earth.

5. When bitten by a Black Mamba, mortality rate is usually 95%.

Comprehension Questions

1. Which snake species are considered to be the largest snakes in the world?

2. Which snake species are considered to be the longest snakes?

3. What do fish and snakes have in common?

4. What do you call the process where the snakes remove or sheds their old skin?

5. What snake is considered to be the deadliest snake in the world?

6. How many venomous snake species are there?

7. What organ is used by snakes to transform air particles into information about their surroundings?

8. Almost all snakes eat meat. What do you call animals which eat only meat?

9. Which snake uses the rattling sound of its tail to warn enemies?

10. What do you call animals such as snakes that cannot adjust their own body temperature?

Comprehension Answers

1. Anaconda
2. Python
3. The don't have eyelids
4. Molting
5. Black Mamba
6. 375
7. Jacobson's organ
8. Carnivores
9. Rattlesnake
10. Cold-blooded

Printed in Great Britain
by Amazon